D0721343

PARAMAHANSA YOGANANDA
(1893–1952)

How-to-Live Series

PARAMAHANSA
YOGANANDA

WHY GOD
PERMITS
EVIL

AND

HOW TO RISE ABOVE IT

Self-Realization Fellowship
FOUNDED 1920
Paramahansa Yogananda

ABOUT THIS BOOK: The lectures in this volume were originally published by Self-Realization Fellowship in its quarterly magazine *Self-Realization,* which was founded by Paramahansa Yogananda in 1925. These talks were given at the Self-Realization Fellowship temples founded by the author in Hollywood and San Diego, California; and were recorded stenographically by Sri Daya Mata, one of Paramahansa Yogananda's earliest and closest disciples.

Copyright © 2002 Self-Realization Fellowship. All rights reserved.
First edition

Authorized by the International Publications Council of
SELF-REALIZATION FELLOWSHIP
3880 San Rafael Avenue
Los Angeles, California 90065-3298

The Self-Realization Fellowship name and emblem (shown above) appear on all SRF books, recordings, and other publications, assuring the reader that a work originates with the society established by Paramahansa Yogananda and faithfully conveys his teachings.

Library of Congress Cataloging-in-Publication Data

Yogananda, Paramahansa, 1893–1952.
  Why God permits evil and how to rise above it / Paramahansa Yogananda.
    p. cm. – (How to live series)
  ISBN 0-87612-461-9 (trade paperback : alk. paper)
1. Self-Realization Fellowship. 2. Spiritual life. 3. Self-realization—Religious aspects. 4. Good and evil. I. Title. II. Series.
  BP605.S4 .Y65 2002
  294.5'2118—dc21

                        2002008198

Printed in the United States of America
13471-54321

Good and evil must ever be complements on this earth. Everything created must bear some guise of imperfection. How else could God, the Sole Perfection, fragment His one consciousness into forms of creation distinguishable from Himself? There can be no images of light without contrasting shadows. Unless evil had been created, man would not know the opposite, good. Night brings out the bright contrast of day; sorrow teaches us the desirability of joy. Though evil must come, woe to him by whom it comes. He who is enticed by delusion to play the villain's part must suffer the villain's sad karmic fate, while the hero receives the hallowed reward of his virtue. Knowing this truth, we must shun evil; becoming good, we ultimately rise to God's high estate — beyond both evil and good.

—Paramahansa Yogananda

CONTENTS

———◆———

PREFACE

"Self-realization is the knowing—in body, mind, and soul—that we are one with the omnipresence of God; that we do not have to pray that it come to us, that we are not merely near it at all times, but that God's omnipresence is our omnipresence; that we are just as much a part of Him now as we ever will be. All we have to do is improve our knowing."

Paramahansa Yogananda

In his "how-to-live" teachings, Paramahansa Yogananda has given to people of all cultures, races, and creeds the means to free themselves from physical, mental, and spiritual inharmonies—to create for themselves a life of enduring happiness and all-round success.

The books in this series present Paramahansaji's how-to-live wisdom on many subjects, providing readers with spiritual insight and practical keys for bringing into daily life the inner balance and harmony that is the essence of yoga. Through the practice of meditation and the universal principles of right action and right attitude highlighted in these books, one can experience every moment as an opportunity to grow in awareness of the Divine.

While each book addresses a distinct topic, one message resonates throughout the series: *Seek God first.* Whether speaking of creating fulfilling relationships, raising spiritual children, overcoming self-defeating habits, or any of the other myriad goals and challenges of modern living, Paramahansa Yogananda again and again refocuses our attention towards life's highest attainment: Self-realization—knowing our true nature as divine beings. Through his inspiration and encouragement, we learn how to live a truly victorious life—transcending limitations, fear, and suffering—by awakening to the infinite power and joy of our real Self: the soul.

— *Self-Realization Fellowship*

Why God Permits Evil
and How to Rise Above It

PART I

Why Evil Is a Part of God's Creation

WHAT IS THE ORIGIN OF EVIL?

Some say that God doesn't know evil, because they can't explain why a God who is good allows robberies, murders, disease, poverty, and other terrible happenings that are going on constantly on this earth. These mis-

---

Extracts from a talk given on November 17, 1946. The complete talk appears in *The Divine Romance* (Paramahansa Yogananda's *Collected Talks and Essays*, Volume II), published by Self-Realization Fellowship.

fortunes are certainly evil to us; but are they evil to God? If they are, why would God permit such evil? And if the evil did not come from Him who is the Supreme Creator of all things, where did it come from? Who created greed? Who created hate? Who created jealousy and anger? Who created harmful bacteria? Who created sex temptation, and the temptation of greed? These were not the invention of human beings. Man could never have experienced them if they had not first been created.

Some people try to explain that evil does not exist, or that it is merely a psychological factor. But this is not so. The evidence of evil is here in the world. You cannot deny it. If there is no evil, why would Jesus pray, "Lead us not into temptation, but deliver us from evil"?* He is saying plainly that evil does exist.

So the truth is, we do find evil in the world.

---

* Matthew 6:13.

And where did it come from? God.* Evil provides the contrast that enables us to recognize and experience goodness. Evil had to be, if there was to be any creation. If you wrote a message with white chalk on a white board, no one would see it. So without the blackboard of evil, the good things in the world could not be magnified at all. For instance, Judas was Jesus' best publicity agent. By his evil act, Judas made Christ eternally famous. Jesus knew the role he had to play, and all that was going to happen to him in order that he might demonstrate the love and greatness of God; and a villain was necessary to this enactment. But it was not good for Judas that he chose to be the one whose dark deed, by contrast, extolled the glories of Christ's triumph over evil.

* "I am the Lord, and there is none else. I form the light, and create darkness: I make peace, and create evil: I the Lord do all these things" (Isaiah 45:6–7).

WHERE IS THE DIVIDING LINE BETWEEN GOOD AND EVIL?

It is hard to know where the dividing line is between good and evil. Certainly it is terrible that bacteria kill two billion people every hundred years. But think of the chaos of overpopulation if there were no death! And if everything here were good and perfect, no one would leave this earth of his own accord; no one would want to go back to God. So in a sense misery is your best friend, because it starts you seeking God. When you begin to see clearly the imperfection of the world, you will begin to seek the perfection of God. The truth is that God is using evil, not to destroy us, but to make us disillusioned with His toys, with the playthings of this world, so that we might seek Him.

This is why the Lord Himself permits injustices and evil. But I have said to Him, "Lord, You have never suffered. You have always been perfect. How do You know what suffering is? Yet You have put us through these tests; and You had no business doing it. We didn't ask to be born as mortals and to suffer." (He doesn't mind that I argue with Him. He is very patient.) The Lord answers, "You don't have to go on suffering; I have given everyone the free will to choose good instead of evil, and thus come back to Me."

So evil is the test of God to see if we will choose Him or His gifts. He created us in His image and gave us the power to free ourselves. But we don't use that power.

THE COSMIC MOTION PICTURE

There is another angle about duality, or good and evil, that I want to explain to you. If a movie producer made motion pictures only of angels, and showed them in the film houses morning, noon, and night every day, he would soon have to close up his business. He has to produce variety in order to attract people's attention. The bad man makes the hero look so much better! And we like plots that are filled with action. We don't mind looking at exciting movies about danger and disaster because we know they are only pictures. I remember one time when I was taken to see a movie in which the hero died; it was such a tragedy! So I stayed and watched the next showing of the picture until I saw the hero alive again; then I left the theater.

If you could see what is going on behind the screen of this life, you wouldn't suffer at all. It is a cosmic motion-picture show. This movie that God is projecting on the screen of this earth has no value to me. I look at the beam of God's light, which is projecting these scenes on the screen of life. I see the pictures of the whole universe coming from this beam.

Another time I was sitting in a movie house watching an exciting drama on the screen. And then I looked into the projection booth. I saw that the projectionist was not interested in the picture, because he had seen it over and over again. Instead, he was reading a book. The projection machine was doing its job: there was the sound, and the beam of light was casting the realistic pictures on the screen. And there was the audience, caught up in the drama. I thought, "Lord, You are like this man sitting here in the booth, absorbed in Your own nature of bliss and love and wisdom. Your machine of cosmic law is throwing on the screen of the universe the scenes of jealousy, of love, of hatred, of wisdom, but You remain uninvolved in Your plays." From age to age, from civilization to civilization, the same old pictures are shown over and over again, only with different characters playing the parts. I think God gets a little bit bored with it all. He is tired of it. It is a wonder that He doesn't just pull the plug and stop the show!

When I took my gaze from the beam of light that was casting the scenes of action on the screen, I looked at the audience in the motion-picture house and I saw that they were going through all the emotions of the actors in the movie. They were suffering with the hero and reacting to the evil of the villain. To the audience it was a tragic experience. To the operator in the projection booth, it was only a picture. And so it is with God. He has created pictures of light and shadows, the hero and the villain, good and evil, and we are the audience and the actors. It is only because we are too much identified with the play that we are in trouble.

Without shadows as well as light there could be no picture. Evil is the shadow that converts the one beam of God's light into pictures or forms. Therefore, evil is the shadow of God that makes this play possible. The dark shadows of evil are interspersed with the pure white beam of the virtues of God. He wants you not to take these pictures so seriously. The director of a movie sees the murders and the suffering and the comedy and the drama as means to create interest for the audience. He stands apart from the play and directs and observes it. God wants us to behave with detachment, realizing we are only actors or observers in His cosmic show.

Though God has everything, we can still say that He has some desire: He wants to see who will remain unintimidated by this picture, and who will play his part well and come back to Him. You can't run away from this universe, but if you act in this play with your thought fixed on God, you will be free.

FOR HIM WHO REALIZES GOD, THERE IS NO EVIL

The way to supreme happiness will not be found by the scientist nor by material-minded people, but by those who follow the masters who say: "Go back to the booth of the Infinite from which you can see the projection of all these cosmic motion pictures. Then you won't be troubled about God's creation, God's play."

My only interest in people is to help them. And as long as breath shall flow in these lungs, so long shall I try to help others and tell them to get away from this motion picture of delusion. Because you are a part of it now, you suffer. You must stand aside and watch it, and then you cannot suffer. When you are an observer, then you can enjoy this play. This is what you must learn. To God, this is only a movie, and when you turn to Him, it will also be a picture show to you.

I will tell you a little story. A king fell asleep

and dreamed that he was poor. He was crying out in his sleep for just a penny for some food. Finally, the queen woke him and said, "What is the matter with you? Your treasury is full of gold, and yet you are crying for a penny."

Then the king said, "Oh, how silly of me. I thought I was a beggar and was starving for lack of that penny."

Such is the delusion of every soul who is dreaming he is a mortal, subject to the nightmarish evils of all kinds of disease, suffering, troubles, heartbreaks. The only way to escape this nightmare is by becoming more attached to God and less attached to the dream images of this world. It is because you have put your attention on the wrong things that you suffer. If you give your heart to man, or drink, or greed, or drugs, you will suffer. Your heart will be broken. You must place your heart with God. The more you seek peace in Him, the more that peace will devour your worries and sufferings.

You suffer because you have allowed yourself to become so susceptible to the evils of this world. You must learn to be spiritually tough, spiritually strong. Do all the things you have to do, and enjoy what you do, but inwardly say, "Lord, I am Thy child, made in Thine image. I don't want anything but You." The devotee who follows this principle, and who attains this realization, will find that for him there is no evil in this world.

"No cruelty exists in God's plan, because in His eyes there is no good or evil — only pictures of light and shadows. The Lord intended us to view the dualistic scenes of life as He does Himself — the ever joyous Witness of a stupendous cosmic drama.

"Man has falsely identified himself with the pseudo-soul or ego. When he transfers his sense of identity to his true being, the immortal soul, he discovers that all pain is unreal. He no longer can even imagine *the state of suffering."*

— Paramahansa Yogananda, in
   Sayings of Paramahansa Yogananda

PART II

Why God Created the World

———❦———

When you are reading a very interesting novel, you see good and evil contradicting each other, and you think it is terrible when evil is winning. For instance, in one chapter the hero is about to be killed; but in the next, everything is straightened out and he is saved. You must understand that each life is a master novel written by God. It is not up to you to try to fathom it; you will be defeated by the limitations of

Extracts from a talk given on December 16, 1945. The complete talk appears in *Journey to Self-realization* (Paramahansa Yogananda's *Collected Talks and Essays*, Volume III), published by Self-Realization Fellowship.

your *maya*-deluded intelligence. First conquer delusion and become one with God; then you will realize why He created this world.*

But we do have a right to ask Him why. And there are many, many reasons. First of all, it could not be that this earth is a necessity to Him, because in that case God would be imperfect; He would have something to attain from it.

---

* *Maya* is the delusory power inherent in the structure of creation, by which the One appears as many. *Maya* is the principle of relativity, inversion, contrast, duality, oppositional states; the "Satan" (lit., in Hebrew, "the adversary") of the Old Testament prophets. Paramahansa Yogananda wrote: "The Sanskrit word *maya* means 'the measurer'; it is the magical power in creation by which limitations and divisions are apparently present in the Immeasurable and Inseparable....In God's plan and play (*lila*), the sole function of Satan or maya is to attempt to divert man from Spirit to matter, from Reality to unreality....*Maya* is the veil of transitoriness in Nature, the ceaseless becoming of creation; the veil that each man must lift in order to see behind it the Creator, the changeless Immutable, eternal Reality."

But we have the testimony of the saints that He is perfect; and I give testimony from my own experience, for I have communed with Him....

THIS WORLD IS GOD'S HOBBY

Since God is perfect and this earth is not a necessity for His evolution, it is therefore a sort of hobby to God. For example, there are two kinds of artists: one type is the commercial artist who makes art pay; and the other type is one who creates gossamer wings of art with no market value, simply for the personal enjoyment of it. Now we cannot think of God as commercial, for He has nothing to gain from His art of creation. Similarly, wealthy people sometimes take up special hobbies that are expensive, because they can afford them. I met such a man in Cincinnati; he had a big farm as his hobby. When I visited there as his guest, I said, "Your farm is not paying for itself, is it?" He replied, "That's right. This egg

I am eating cost me ninety cents. I could get one in the market for a few pennies."

So this world is God's hobby. But it is not any fun for those who are suffering in it. I often say to the Lord, "If You wanted a hobby, why did You create pain and cancer and terrible emotions as part of it?" Of course, I am not in the world to dictate to the Lord. I know that. But I humbly fight with Him.

He laughs at me, and says, "In the last chapter, all will know the answer to these questions."

Well, I know the answer, but I argue on behalf of those who don't: "It may be a play to You, Lord, but it is misery and death to those who don't know it is just a play. Two people marry and think they have found perfect love, and then one of them dies — what a tragedy! Or someone who has made lots of money thinks he is happy and then sees the stock market crash, and in despair jumps out the window — how terrible! And in the sense traps of sex, wine, and money there is temptation not only from outside, but from within. How is man going to justify all this? And why are there gangsters, and persons who are insane, and all kinds of dreadful goings-on, Lord? Why are there germs that kill so many people every year? If the bones of those who die of disease were heaped together, the pile would be as high as the Himalayas; and yet it is a hobby to You, God. What about those who are victims of Your hobby?"

And the Lord says, "I have made all men in My image. If you know you are a part of Me, you can live in this world and enjoy it as I do."

That is the ultimate answer. We do not see this world as God sees it.

Seeing With the Open Eyes of Wisdom and Calmness

I will give you an example of how things went wrong in creation. If right now in this room I suddenly close my eyes and start danc-

17

ing wildly, forgetting everything around me and the limitations of my blindness, you will call out to me, "Be careful! You will fall or bump something!" But I insist, "No, I am all right." Then I do stumble and fall and break my leg; and I cry and ask, "Why did this happen to me?" You will answer, "Well, why did you close your eyes and try to dance in the darkness?" Then I reply, "Oh, my goodness. Why did I dance with my eyes closed?"

Because your eyes are closed, you cannot help thinking this world is terrible. But if you keep open your eyes of wisdom and calmness, you will see there is a lot of enjoyment in this world — just as though you are watching a motion picture....

WE HAVE FREE CHOICE TO BECOME ENTANGLED IN THE DRAMA OR TO RISE ABOVE IT

We can say that God made this earth not

only as a hobby, but also because He wanted to make perfect souls that would evolve back to Him. He sent them out under the cloak of delusion, or *maya,* but endowed with freedom. That is the greatest gift of God. He has not denied mankind the free choice that He Himself has. He has given man freedom to be good or evil, to do exactly as he pleases — even to deny God. Both good and evil exist, but nobody compels you to be evil unless you choose to practice evil; and nobody can compel you to be good unless you want to be good. God created us with the ability to exercise His gifts of intelligence and free choice, by which we can choose to go back to Him. God certainly means to take us back when we are ready to go. We are like the biblical prodigal son, and God is continuously calling to us to come Home.

The ideal of every human life should be to be good, to be happy, and to find God. You will never be happy unless you do find God. That is why Jesus said, "Seek ye first the kingdom of God."* That is the purpose of our existence: that we strive to become good, to become perfect, and to use our free will to choose good instead of evil. God has given to us all the power we need to do so. The mind is like an elastic band. The more you pull, the more it stretches. The mind-elastic will never break. Every time you feel limitations, close your eyes and say to yourself, "I am the Infinite," and you will see what power you have.

No joy of the senses, no joy of possession, can match the joy of God. Though He had everything from eternity to eternity, He began to think, "I am all-powerful, and Joy itself, but there is no one else to enjoy Me." And He thought, as He began to create: "I will make souls in My image, and clothe them as human

* Matthew 6:33.

beings with free choice, to see whether they will seek My material gifts and the temptations of money, wine, and sex; or whether they will seek the million million times more intoxicating joy of My consciousness." The point that gives me the most satisfaction is that God is very just and fair. He gave man freedom to accept His love and live in His joy, or to cast it aside and live in delusion, in ignorance of Him.

Though all created things belong to God, there is one thing God hasn't — our love. When He created us, He did have something to attain, and that is our love. We can withhold that love, or give it to Him. And He will wait endlessly until we are ready to offer our love to Him. When we do, when the prodigal son comes Home, the fatted calf of wisdom is killed and there is much rejoicing. When a soul returns to God, there actually is rejoicing among all the saints in heaven. This is the meaning of the parable of the prodigal son as told by Jesus.

WATCH YOURSELF FROM THE BALCONY OF INTROSPECTION

There is so much more to life than what you think. Since everything earthly seems so real, how much more so must be the Reality that creates this unreal reality! But the unreal reality makes you forget the Real. God wants you to remember that you wouldn't mind this earth if it were like a motion picture. Even if the brittle bones of the body break, you would say, "Well, look at those broken bones," and not feel any disturbance or suffering. You can say that when you are anchored in the Divine Consciousness. You will make fun of your habits, and you will be intensely amused at your distinguishing characteristics, as from the balcony of introspection you watch yourself perform in the motion picture of life. I do that all the time. When you know this world to be God's *lila* — His play — then you aren't upset by the contrasts in this drama of good and evil.

In a dream you can behold rich people, poor people, someone strong, someone else groaning with disease, someone dying, and someone being born. But when you wake up, you realize that it was only a dream. This universe is God's dream. And when I ask Him, "Why do You not dream only beautiful dreams? Why must Your play be fraught with nightmares?" He replies, "You must be able to enjoy both the nightmares and the beautiful experiences for what they are — dreams, only dreams. But if you dream only beautiful dreams, you will be drowned in that beauty, and never wish to wake up." That is the answer. So you must not be frightened when nightmares come, but say, "Lord, it is a passing dream. It has no reality." And when you are smiling with health and happiness, say, "Lord, it is a beautiful dream, but do what You like with my dreams of life." When you are neither touched by the nightmares of disease and suffering and worries, nor bound by the beautiful dreams, then God says, "Wake up, now! Come back Home."

SEPARATE THE UNREAL FROM THE REAL

As a little boy, I used to dream that a tiger was after me; I would cry out that the tiger had caught my leg. Mother would come and shake me from my dream and say, "See, there is nothing wrong. There is no tiger. Your leg is all right." As a result of that childhood dream I had the first wonderful experience that God gave to me: The last time I had that dream, I said, "That is an old trick. There is no tiger after my leg." And I quickly jumped out of the dream. It went away and never returned. From that time on I was watchful, even in dreams, to separate the unreal from the Real.

Saints are those who are half awake and half dreaming: on one side awake in God, and on the other side dreaming the dream of incarnation. But they can quickly get out of this dream. When my body feels some hurt or pain, I focus my eyes and my mind here at the *Kutastha*, or Christ-consciousness center, between the eyebrows, and then I feel no pain; and in a little while I don't even see or feel the body.*

So remember, God is dreaming this world. And if we are in tune with Him, we will live a divinely intoxicated life and nothing will disturb us. We will watch this cosmic picture as we watch the films in a movie house, without being hurt. God created us that we may dream as He does, enjoying this dream, and all its

---

* "Christ Consciousness" is the projected consciousness of God immanent in all creation. In Christian scripture it is called the "only begotten son," the only pure reflection in creation of God the Father; in Hindu scripture it is called *Kutastha Chaitanya* or *Tat*, the cosmic intelligence of Spirit everywhere present in creation. It is the universal consciousness, oneness with God, manifested by Jesus, Krishna, and other avatars. Great saints and yogis know it as the state of *samadhi* meditation wherein their consciousness has become identified with the intelligence in every particle of creation; they feel the entire universe as their own body.

contrasting experiences, as an entertainment, without being affected by it, absorbed in His eternal joy.

———✦———

"'Know ye not that ye are the temple of God, and that the Spirit of God dwelleth in you?'* If you can clarify and expand your mind through meditation, and receive God in your consciousness, you too will be free from the delusion of disease, limitations, and death."

— Paramahansa Yogananda, in
The Divine Romance

* I Corinthians 3:16.

An answered prayer...

One day I entered a cinema house to view a newsreel of the European battlefields. The First World War was still being waged in the West; the newsreel presented the carnage with such realism that I left the theater with a troubled heart.

"Lord," I prayed, "why dost Thou permit such suffering?"

To my intense surprise, an instant answer came in the form of a vision of the actual European battlefields. The scenes, filled with the dead and dying, far surpassed in ferocity any representation of the newsreel.

"Look intently!" A gentle Voice spoke to my inner consciousness. "You will see that these scenes now being enacted in France are nothing but a play of chiaroscuro. They are the cosmic motion picture, as real and as unreal as the theater newsreel you have just seen — a play within a play."

My heart was still not comforted. The Divine Voice went on: "Creation is light and shadow both, else no picture is possible. The good and evil of *maya* must ever alternate in supremacy. If joy were ceaseless here in this world, would man ever desire another? Without suffering, he scarcely cares to recall that he has forsaken his eternal home. Pain is a prod to remembrance. The way of escape is through wisdom. The tragedy of death is unreal; those who shudder at it are like an ignorant actor who dies of fright on the stage when nothing more has been fired at him than a blank cartridge. My sons are children of light; they will not sleep forever in delusion."

Although I had read scriptural accounts of *maya*, they had not given me the deep insight that came with personal visions and with the accompanying words of consolation. One's values are profoundly changed when he is finally convinced that creation is only a vast motion picture; and that not in it, but beyond it, lies his own reality.

— Paramahansa Yogananda, in
Autobiography of a Yogi

"*Yoga is that science by which the soul gains mastery over the instruments of body and mind and uses them to attain Self-realization — the reawakened consciousness of its transcendent, immortal nature, one with Spirit. As an individualized self, the soul has descended from the universality of Spirit and become identified with the limitations of the body and its sense-consciousness....*

"*When you change the center of consciousness, perception, and feeling from the body and mind to the soul — your true, immortal, transcendental Self — you will have the yogi's mastery over life and victory over death.*"

— Paramahansa Yogananda

PART III

A World of Cosmic Entertainment

THE WORLD IS GOD'S DIVINE PLAY

The *rishis* of ancient India, having penetrated to the Original Cause of Being, declare that God is perfect; that He needs nothing, for all is contained within Himself; and that this world is God's *lila*, or divine play. The

Extracts from a talk given on December 9, 1945. The complete talk appears in *Journey to Self-realization* (Paramahansa Yogananda's *Collected Talks and Essays*, Volume III), published by Self-Realization Fellowship.

Lord, it seems, like a little child, loves to play, and His *lila* is the endless variety of ever-changing creation.

I used to reason in this way: God was infinite omniscient Bliss; but, being alone, there was no one but Him to enjoy that Bliss. So He said, "Let Me create a universe and divide Myself into many souls that they may play with Me in My unfolding drama." By His magical measuring power of *maya* He became dual: Spirit and Nature, man and woman, positive and negative.* But even though He has created the universe out of delusion, He Himself is not deluded by it. He knows that everything is but a diversification of His one Cosmic Consciousness. Experiences of the senses and emotions, the dramas of war and peace, sickness and health, life and death—all are happening in God as the Dreamer-Creator of all things, but He is unaffected by them. One

* See footnote on *maya*, page 14.

part of His Infinite Being ever remains transcendent, beyond vibratory dualities: there God is inactive. When He vibrates His consciousness with thoughts of diversity, He becomes immanent and omnipresent as the Creator in the finite vibratory realm of infinity: there He is active. Vibration brings forth objects and beings interacting in space in the motions of time—just as vibrations of man's consciousness bring forth dreams in sleep.

IF WE UNITE OURSELVES WITH GOD, WE WILL NO LONGER SUFFER

God created this dream universe for entertaining Himself and us. The only objection I have to God's *lila* is this: "Lord, why did You permit suffering to be a part of the play?" Pain is so ugly and torturing. Existence then is no longer entertainment, but a tragedy. That is where the intercession of the saints comes in. They remind us that God is all-powerful, and if we unite ourselves with Him, we will no longer be hurt in this playhouse of His. It is we who inflict pain on ourselves if we transgress the divine laws on which He rests the whole universe. Our salvation is to unite with Him. Unless we attune ourselves to God and know thereby that this world is but a cosmic entertainment, we are bound to suffer. It seems that suffering is a necessary discipline to remind us to seek union with God. Then, like Him, we will be entertained by this fantastic play.

It is wondrous to think deeply of these things. I delve in these realms all the time. Even as I speak to you I am seeing these truths. It would indeed be terrible if an Almighty Being had thrown us into this delusive earthly existence without an escape or the ability to realize what He realizes. But this is not the case. There is an outlet. Every night in deep sleep you unconsciously forget this world; it is no more for you. And every time

you meditate deeply, you are consciously transcendent; the world doesn't exist for you.
Thus do the saints say that to unite ourselves
with God is the only way we can understand
that this world is not something to which we
should give much importance....

IF YOU KNEW YOUR IMMORTAL NATURE, YOU WOULDN'T MIND THIS DRAMA

We can say that God should never have
created this world in which there is so much
trouble. But on the other hand, the saints
say that if you knew you were gods,* you
wouldn't mind it. If you watch a movie, you
like a lot of action rather than something dull,
don't you? That is the way you should enjoy
this world. Look upon life as a movie, and
then you will know why God created it. Our

---

* "Is it not written in your law, I said, Ye are gods?"
(John 10:34).

problem is that we forget to see it as God's entertainment.

Through scripture, God has said that we are made in His image. As such, we could behold this world drama as a movie, even as He does, if we but look to that soul perfection within and realize our unity with the Divine. Then this cosmic movie, with its horrors of disease and poverty and atomic bombs, will appear to us only as real as the anomalies we experience in a movie house. When we have finished seeing the motion picture, we know that nobody was killed; nobody was suffering. In fact, that truth is the only answer I see when I look at the drama of life. It is nothing but an electrical shadow-show, a play of light and shadows. Everything is the vibration of God's consciousness condensed into electromagnetic images. The essence of those images cannot be severed by a sword, nor burned, nor drowned, nor suffer pain of any sort. It is not born nor does it die. It only passes through a few changes.* If we could watch this world as God watches it, and as the saints do, we would be free from the seeming reality of this dreaming....

AWAKEN FROM THE COSMIC DREAM

Just as when you are half awake and can see a dream and know you are dreaming, yet apart from it, that is how God feels this universe. On one side He is awake in ever new Bliss, and on another side He is dreaming this universe. That

---

* "This Self is never born nor does it ever perish; nor having come into existence will it again cease to be. It is birthless, eternal, changeless, ever-same (unaffected by the usual processes associated with time). It is not slain when the body is killed....

"No weapon can pierce the soul; no fire can burn it; no water can moisten it; nor can any wind wither it. The soul is uncleavable; it cannot be burnt or wetted or dried. The soul is immutable, all-permeating, ever calm, and immovable—eternally the same" (*God Talks With Arjuna: The Bhagavad Gita* II:20, 23–24).

is how you should look upon this world. Then you will know why He created it, and you will not ascribe these dream conditions to your soul. If you pass through a nightmare, you know that it is no more than a bad dream. If you can live in the world in that consciousness, you will not suffer. That is what *Kriya Yoga* will give to you. That is what *Self-Realization Fellowship Lessons* will do for you if you practice them faithfully.* It is on these teachings that you should concentrate, not on my personality or any other personality. And it is not a matter of merely reading these truths, but of practicing them. Reading does not make you wise; realization does.

That is why I don't read much. I keep my mind always here at the Christ Consciousness

---

* *Kriya Yoga* is a sacred spiritual science, originating millenniums ago in India. It includes certain techniques of meditation whose devoted practice leads to realization of God, taught to students of the *Self-Realization Fellowship Lessons.*

(*Kutastha*) center. In the omnipresent light of Cosmic Intelligence how different the world appears! Sometimes I see everything as electrical images; there is no weight or mass to the body. Reading the wonders of science will not make you a sage, for there is so much more to be known. Read from the book of life that is hidden within, in the omniscience of the soul, just behind the darkness of closed eyes. Discover that boundless realm of Reality. Look upon this earth as a dream, and then you will understand that it is all right for you to lie down on the bed of this earth and dream the dream of life. You won't mind then, because you will know you are dreaming.

Western religious teachers preach prosperity, happiness, health, and the promise of a glorious afterlife; but not how to experience Divine Bliss and be untouched by suffering in the here and now. That is where the teachings of the great *rishis* of India go much deeper.

Occidentals have accused the masters of propounding a negative philosophy of life—that is, never mind whether you suffer, never mind whether you are happy or not; deny the world. On the contrary, the masters of India ask, "What are you going to do when you are confronted with pain and sorrow? Are you going to cry helplessly, or are you going to practice those techniques that give evenmindedness and transcendence while you are treating the malady?" They urge commonsense remedial action and simultaneous control of the emotions so that if health does go away and pain comes you do not give in to despair. In other words, they stress the importance of enthroning oneself within in the unalloyed happiness of the soul, which cannot be tarnished by the whimsical winds of beautiful dreams of life nor by the corrosive storms of nightmares. Those who habitually cling to material consciousness do not want to make the effort required to reach that state of invulnerability. When suffering comes, they do not learn from it and so repeat the same mistakes....

Do not pay undue attention to the passing scenes of life. You are the immortal Self, living only temporarily in a dream that is sometimes a nightmare. That is the higher philosophy of the masters of India.

EMOTIONAL SENSITIVITY IS THE CAUSE OF SUFFERING

Do not be so sensitive. Emotional sensitivity is the silent cause of all suffering. To give strength to creation as a reality by emotional involvement in it is foolishness. To not meditate, to not sit still and realize your true soul nature, but to drift along as a part of the eternal motion of creation, is a constant danger to your happiness. Perhaps some day your body will be terribly sick, and though you want to walk or do other things that you used to do in your younger or healthier days, you find you cannot do them; it is a terrible disillusionment for the soul. Before that day comes, make yourself so free that you can look on your body with detachment, caring for it as though it were somebody else's.

One of my students had a very painful condition in her knee in which the bones were decaying. I don't know how many times that leg was operated upon and put back together again. But she talked of it as though it were nothing: "It is a minor operation," she would say casually. Now that is the way to take life. Cultivate that state of mind by which you can live with greater mental strength.

Even when you do not have the opportunity to meditate long or deeply, always think that you are working for God. When your mind can remain anchored in Him, you will not suffer anymore; no amount of disease or illness will be able to touch you inwardly. Sometimes when this body gives trouble, I look within and everything vanishes in the light of God. Just as you see the moving pictures on the screen and enjoy the contrasting conflict between good and evil actions and between the joyful and sorrowful scenarios, so you shall be entertained by this world. You shall say, "Lord, whatever You do is all right." But until you consciously realize that this is all a dream, you will not see why God created this world.

BE LIKE THE ACTIVE-INACTIVE LORD

I think that in bringing forth the universe God wanted to keep busy. Let this be an incentive to spiritual aspirants. Many think that to find God and get away from this dream they have to forsake their responsibilities and seek seclusion in the Himalayas or other such totally solitary places; but that is not so simple. The mind will still be absorbed in its moods and restlessness, and the body will have to be very active just to keep warm and satisfy its hunger and other needs. It is easier to find God in the jungle of civilization if you follow a balance between meditation and constructive, dutiful work. Be like the active-inactive Lord. In creation He is joyously busy; beyond creation He is joyously quiescent in divine bliss. Because I made the effort to find God in meditation, I am enjoying His bliss even in the midst of activity. And thus activity doesn't adversely affect me at all. Even though I may say I don't like this or that in the dualities around me, still within I am calm and like steel: "Calmly active and actively calm; a prince of peace sitting on the throne of poise directing the kingdom of activity."

To all appearances, it seems that out of perfection God created imperfect beings. But in truth, imperfect beings are perfect — souls made in God's image. All God wants you to do is separate your dream imperfections from your perfect Self. When you think about your mortal life and all your troubles and identify with them, you do an injustice to the image of God within you. Affirm and realize, "I am not a mortal being; I am Spirit."

THROUGH EVIL AS WELL AS GOOD, GOD IS COAXING US BACK TO HIM

God is ever trying to draw His children back to their inherent perfection. That is why you will see even in evil people there is a search for God, though it may not be pronounced as such. Can you find an evil person who wants to derive misery from his actions? No. He thinks his pursuits are going to give him a good time. The man who drinks or takes dope thinks he will get pleasure from it. Everywhere you will see people, good and evil, searching in their own way for happiness. No one wants to hurt himself. Then why do people behave in an evil way that is bound to cause pain and sorrow? Such actions arise from the greatest of all sins — ignorance. "Wrongdoer" is the right word rather than "sinner." You may condemn wrongdoing but should not condemn the doer. Sins are errors committed under the influence of ignorance, or delusion. But for a different degree of understanding, you might be in the same boat. Jesus said, "He that is without sin among you, let him cast a stone."*

The point is, in everything we do we are seeking happiness. No one can truthfully say he is a materialist, because anyone who is seeking happiness is seeking God. Therefore, in evil as well as in good God is coaxing us back to Him by our search for happiness. The sorrow inflicted by evil will eventually turn the wayward to the joys of virtue. Since life is inherently a medley of good and evil, of beautiful dreams and nightmares, we should seek out and help to create the beautiful dreams and not get caught up in the frightful nightmares.

*John 8:7.

To Know God Is True Wisdom

In reacting to life, most people either say, "Praise the Lord," or urge us to be afraid of Him; and some blame or curse Him. I think this is very foolish. What can you say to God that will be praise? He is not moved by praise or flattery, because He has everything. Most prayers are offered by people who are in trouble; some cry out, "Praise the Lord," hoping for some favor thereby. You may curse or praise the Lord; it will not make any difference to Him. But it will make a difference in you. Praise Him—or better still, *love* Him—and you will feel better. Curse Him and it reacts to hurt you. When you go against God, you are going against your own true nature, the divine image in which God created you. When you go against that nature, you automatically punish yourself.

From my childhood I was rebellious at life, because I saw so much injustice. But now the

47

only rebellion I feel within me is that people do not know God. The greatest sin is ignorance — not to know what life is all about. And the greatest virtue is wisdom — to know the meaning and purpose of life and its Creator. To know that we are not little human beings, but that we are one with Him, is wisdom.

Every night in sleep God takes away all of your troubles to show you that you are not a mortal being; you are Spirit. God wants you to remember that truth during the conscious state, so that you are not bothered any more by the anomalies of life. If we can very well exist at night in deep sleep without thinking about this world and its troubles, we can very well exist in God's world of activity without being caught up in this dream. Even though dream universes are floating in God's consciousness, He is ever awake and knows He is dreaming. He tells us, "Do not get panicky during this daydream; look to Me as the

Reality behind the dream." When there is health and joy, smile in the dream. When there is a nightmare of sickness or sorrow, say, "I am awake in God, merely watching the play of my life." Then you will know that God has created this universe as an entertainment for Himself. And you, being made in His image, have not only the perfect right but also the ability to enjoy this play with its varying dreams even as He does....

Dismiss this phantasma of disease and health, sorrow and joy. Rise above it. Become the Self. Watch the show of the universe, but do not become absorbed in it. Many times I have seen my body gone from this world. I laugh at death. I am ready anytime. There is nothing to it. Eternal life is mine. I am the ocean of consciousness. Sometimes I become the little wave of the body, but I am never just the wave without the Ocean of God.

Death and darkness cannot cast fear upon

us, for we are the very Consciousness out of which this universe has been created by God.

In the Bhagavad Gita the Lord says:

> *Whoever realizes Me to be the Unborn and Beginningless as well as the Sovereign Lord of Creation—that man has conquered delusion and attained the sinless state even while wearing a mortal body....*
>
> *I am the Source of everything; from Me all creation emerges. With this realization the wise, awestricken, adore Me. Their thoughts fully on Me, their beings surrendered to Me, enlightening one another, proclaiming Me always, My devotees are contented and joyful....*
>
> *From sheer compassion I, the Divine Indweller, set alight in them the radiant lamp of wisdom which banishes the darkness that is born of ignorance.*
>
> — Bhagavad Gita X:3, 8–9,11.

PART IV

Discovering God's Unconditional Love Behind the Mystery-Veil of Creation

---

No man, no prophet, will ever be able to wipe away all the inequalities and divisions on this earth. But when you will find yourself in the consciousness of God, these differences will vanish and you will say:

Oh, life is sweet and death a dream,
When Thy song flows through me.

Selections from lectures by Paramahansa Yogananda.

Then joy is sweet, sorrow a dream,
When Thy song flows through me.
Then health is sweet, sickness a dream,
When Thy song flows through me.
Then praise is sweet and blame a dream,
When Thy song flows through me.*

This is the highest philosophy. Do not be afraid of anything. Even when tossing on a wave in a storm, you are still on the bosom of the ocean. Always hold on to the consciousness of God's underlying presence. Be of even mind, and say: "I am fearless; I am made of the substance of God. I am a spark of the Fire of Spirit. I am an atom of the Cosmic Flame. I am a cell of the vast universal body of the Father. 'I and my Father are One.'"

———◆———

* These lines are from a song in *Cosmic Chants* by Paramahansa Yogananda (published by Self-Realization Fellowship).

Use all the strength of your soul to find God....The smoke-screen of delusion has come between us and Him, and He is sorry that we have lost sight of Him. He is not happy seeing His children suffer so much—dying from falling bombs, terrible diseases, and wrong habits of living. He regrets it, for He loves us and wants us back. If only you would make the effort at night to meditate and be with Him! He thinks of you so much. You are not forsaken. It is you who have forsaken your Self....God is never indifferent to you....

The sole purpose of creation is to compel you to solve its mystery and perceive God behind all. He wants you to forget everything else and to seek Him alone. Once you have found refuge in the Lord, there is no consciousness of life and death as realities. You will then see all dualities like dreams during sleep, coming and going in the eternal existence of God. Forget not this sermon, a sermon He is expressing to you through my voice. Forget not! He is saying:

"I am just as helpless as you, for I, as your soul, am tied in the body with you. Unless you redeem your Self, I am caged with you. Dally no more, groveling in the mud of suffering and ignorance. Come! bathe in My light."

❖

The Lord wants us to escape this delusive world. He cries for us, for He knows how hard it is for us to gain His deliverance. But you have only to remember that you are His child. Don't pity yourself. You are loved just as much by God as are Jesus and Krishna. You must seek His love, for it encompasses eternal freedom, endless joy, and immortality.

❖

Just beneath the shadows of this life is God's wondrous Light. The universe is a vast temple of His presence. When you meditate, you will find doors opening to Him everywhere. When you have communion with Him, not all the ravages of the world can take away that Joy and Peace.

ABOUT THE AUTHOR

PARAMAHANSA YOGANANDA (1893–1952) is widely regarded as one of the preeminent spiritual figures of our time. Born in northern India, he came to the United States in 1920, where for more than thirty years he taught India's ancient science of meditation and the art of balanced spiritual living. Through his acclaimed life story, *Autobiography of a Yogi,* and his numerous other books, Paramahansa Yogananda has introduced millions of readers to the perennial wisdom of the East. Under the guidance of one of his earliest and closest disciples, Sri Daya Mata, his spiritual and humanitarian work is carried on by Self-Realization Fellowship, the international society he founded in 1920 to disseminate his teachings worldwide.

A World in Transition: Finding Spiritual Security in Times of Change *(Anthology—Paramahansa Yogananda and other monastics of Self-Realization Fellowship)*

Self-Realization Fellowship Lessons

The scientific techniques of meditation taught by Paramahansa Yogananda, including *Kriya Yoga*—as well as his guidance on all aspects of balanced spiritual living—are presented in the *Self-Realization Fellowship Lessons*. For further information, you are welcome to write for the free booklet, *Undreamed-of Possibilities*.

SELF-REALIZATION FELLOWSHIP
3880 San Rafael Avenue • Los Angeles, CA 90065-3298
TEL (323) 225-2471 • FAX (323) 225-5088

www.yogananda-srf.org